LAW,
LIBERTY,
AND
MORALITY

LAW, LIBERTY, AND MORALITY

H. L. A. Hart

VINTAGE BOOKS

A Division of Random House

NEW YORK

CONTENTS

I

The Legal Enforcement of Morality, 1
Conspiracy to Corrupt Public Morals, 6
Prostitution and Homosexuality, 13
Positive and Critical Morality, 17

II

The Use and Abuse of Examples, 25
Paternalism and the Enforcement of Morality, 30
The Moral Gradation of Punishment, 34
Private Immorality and Public Indecency, 38
The Moderate and the Extreme Thesis, 48

III

Varieties of Enforcement, 53
Retribution and Denunciation, 60
The Preservation of Morality and Moral Conservatism, 69
Moral Populism and Democracy, 77
Conclusion, 81

Selected Bibliography, 85
Index, 87

I

THE LEGAL ENFORCEMENT OF MORALITY

These lectures are concerned with one question about the relations between law and morals. I say, advisedly, "one question," because in the heat of the controversy often generated when law and morals are mentioned in conjunction, it is often overlooked that there is not just one question concerning their relations but many different questions needing quite separate consideration. So I shall start by distinguishing four such questions and identifying the one with which I shall be here concerned.

The first is a historical and a causal question: Has the development of the law been influenced by morals? The answer to this question plainly is "Yes"; though of course this does not mean that an affirmative answer may not also be given to the converse question: Has the development of morality been influenced by law? This latter question has scarcely been adequately investigated yet, but there are now many admirable American and English studies of the former question. These exhibit the manifold ways in which morality has determined the course of the law, sometimes covertly and slowly through the judicial process, sometimes openly and abruptly through legislation. I shall say no more here about this historical causal question, except to utter the warning that the affirmative answer which may be given to it, and to its converse, does not mean that an affirmative answer is to be given to other quite different questions about the relations of law and morals.

The second question may be called an analytical or definitional one. Must some reference to morality enter into an adequate definition of law or legal system? Or is it just a contingent fact that law and morals often overlap (as in their common proscription of certain forms of violence and dishonesty) and that they share a common vocabulary of rights, obligations, and duties? These are famous questions in the long history of the philosophy of law, but perhaps they are not so important as the amount of time and ink expended upon them suggests. Two things have conspired to make discussion of them interminable or seemingly so. The first is that the issue has been clouded by use of grand but vague words like "Positivism" and "Natural Law." Banners have been waved and parties formed in a loud but often confused debate. Secondly, amid the shouting, too little has been said about the criteria for judging the adequacy of a definition of law. Should such a definition state what, if anything, the plain man intends to convey when he uses the expressions "law" or "legal system"? Or should it rather aim to provide, by marking off certain social phenomena from others, a classification useful or illuminating for theoretical purposes?

A third question concerns the possibility and the forms of the moral criticism of law. Is law open to moral criticism? Or does the admission that a rule is a valid legal rule preclude moral criticism or condemnation of it by reference to moral standards or principles? Few perhaps of this audience would find any contradiction or paradox in the assertion that a rule of law was valid and yet conflicted with some binding moral principle requiring behaviour contrary to that demanded by the legal rule. Yet in our own day Kelsen[1] has argued that there is a logical contradiction in such an assertion, unless it is interpreted merely as an autobiographical statement or psychological report by the speaker of his divergent inclinations both to obey the law and to disobey it by following the moral principle.

Within this third question there are many subordinate ones. Even if we admit, as most would, the possibility of a moral criticism of law, we may ask whether there are any forms of moral criticism which are uniquely or exclusively relevant to law. Does criticism in terms of Justice exhaust all the relevant forms? Or does "good law" mean something different from and wider than "just law"? Is

[1] Hans Kelsen, *General Theory of Law and State,* pp. 374–76, 407–10.

3

Justice, as Bentham seems to have thought, merely a name for the efficient distribution of Utility or Welfare, or is it otherwise reducible to them? Plainly the adequacy of Utilitarianism as a moral critique of social institutions is in issue here.

The fourth question is the subject of these lectures. It concerns the legal enforcement of morality and has been formulated in many different ways: Is the fact that certain conduct is by common standards immoral sufficient to justify making that conduct punishable by law? Is it morally permissible to enforce morality as such? Ought immorality as such to be a crime?

To this question John Stuart Mill gave an emphatic negative answer in his essay *On Liberty* one hundred years ago, and the famous sentence in which he frames this answer expresses the central doctrine of his essay. He said, "The only purpose for which power can rightfully be exercised over any member of a civilised community against his will is to prevent harm to others."[2] And to identify the many different things which he intended to exclude, he added, "His own good either physical or moral is not a sufficient warrant. He cannot rightfully be compelled to do or forbear because it will be better for him to do so, because it will make him happier, because in the opinions of others, to do so would be wise or even right."[3]

This doctrine, Mill tells us, is to apply to human beings

[2] *On Liberty,* Chapter 1.   [3] *Ibid.*

only "in the maturity of their faculties": it is not to apply to children or to backward societies. Even so, it has been the object of much academic criticism on two different, and indeed inconsistent, grounds. Some critics have urged that the line which Mill attempts to draw between actions with which the law may interfere and those with which it may not is illusory. "No man is an island"; and in an organised society it is impossible to identify classes of actions which harm no one or no one but the individual who does them. Other critics have admitted that such a division of actions may be made, but insist that it is merely dogmatic on Mill's part to limit legal coercion to the class of actions which harm others. There are good reasons, so these critics claim, for compelling conformity to social morality and for punishing deviations from it even when these do not harm others.

I shall consider this dispute mainly in relation to the special topic of sexual morality where it seems *prima facie* plausible that there are actions immoral by accepted standards and yet not harmful to others. But to prevent misunderstanding I wish to enter a *caveat*; I do not propose to defend all that Mill said; for I myself think there may be grounds justifying the legal coercion of the individual other than the prevention of harm to others. But on the narrower issue relevant to the enforcement of morality Mill seems to me to be right. It is of course possible simply to assert that the legal enforcement by society of its accepted morality needs no argument to justify it, because it is a morality which is enforced. But Mill's critics have not fallen back upon this brute assertion. They have in fact advanced many different arguments to justify the enforcement of morality, but these all, as I shall attempt to show, rest on unwarranted assumptions as to matters of fact, or on certain evaluations whose plausibility, due in large measure to ambiguity or vagueness or inaccuracy of statement, dwindles (even if it does not altogether vanish) when exposed to critical scrutiny.

CONSPIRACY TO CORRUPT PUBLIC MORALS

In England in the last few years the question whether the criminal law should be used to punish immorality "as such" has acquired a new practical importance; for there has, I think, been a revival there of what might be termed *legal moralism.* Judges both in their judicial capacity and in extra-judicial statements have gone out of their way to express the view that the enforcement of sexual morality is a proper part of the law's business—as much its business, so one judge has argued, as the suppression of treason. It is not clear what has provoked this resurgence of legal moralism: there must have been many factors at work, and among them, perhaps, has been the idea that a general stiffening of the sanctions attached to any form of immorality may be one way to meet the general increase in crime by which we are all vastly disturbed. But whatever its cause, this movement of judicial opinion has gone far. Last year the House of Lords in the case of *Shaw* v. *Director of Public Prosecutions*[4] conjured up, from what many had thought was its grave the eighteenth century, the conception (itself a creature of the Star Chamber) that "a conspiracy to corrupt public morals" is a common law offence. As a result of this decision the prosecuting authorities in England can now face their complex problems equipped with Lord Mansfield's dictum of 1774 which some of the judges in Shaw's case invoked in their speeches.

> Whatever is *contra bonos mores et decorum* the principles of our laws prohibit and the King's Court as the general censor and guardian of the public morals is bound to restrain and punish.[5]

Of course the penal code of California, like that of many states of the Union, includes in its calendar of crimes a conspiracy to injure public morals, and it may seem strange to Americans to hear the recognition of this offence by the English House of Lords represented as a new development. But Americans are accustomed, as the English are not, to the inclusion among their statutes of much legal lumber in the form of penal provisions no longer enforced, and I am assured that, in California at least, the provision making a conspiracy to corrupt public morals a crime may safely

[4] (1961) 2 A.E.R. 446. (1962) A.C. 223.
[5] Jones v. Randall (1774). Lofft. at p. 385.

be regarded as a dead letter. This is now not so with the English, and both the use actually made of the law in Shaw's case and the future use envisaged for it by the House of Lords are worth consideration.

The facts in Shaw's case are not such as to excite sympathy for the accused. What Shaw had done was to compose and procure the publication of a magazine called the *Ladies Directory* giving the names and addresses of prostitutes, in some cases nude photographs, and an indication in code of their practices. For this Shaw was charged and found guilty of three offences: (1) publishing an obscene article, (2) living on the earnings of the prostitutes who paid for the insertion of their advertisements in the *Ladies Directory*, (3) conspiring to corrupt public morals by means of the *Ladies Directory*.

All this may seem a somewhat ponderous three-handed engine to use merely to ensure the conviction and imprisonment of Shaw; but English law has always preferred the policy of thorough. The judges in the House of Lords not only raised no objection to the inclusion of the charge of conspiracy to corrupt public morals, but with one dissentient (Lord Reid) they confirmed the prosecution's contention that this was an offence still known to English law and insisted that it was a salutary thing that this should be so. They made indeed an excursion, rare for English judges, into the area of policy in order to emphasise this.

To show the contemporary need for the newly resuscitated penal law one of the judges (Lord Simonds), a former Lord Chancellor, made the following remarkable statement:

> When Lord Mansfield speaking long after the Star Chamber had been abolished said that the Court of King's Bench was the *custos morum* of the people and had the superintendency of offences *contra bonos mores,* he was asserting, as I now assert, that there is in that Court a residual power, where no statute has yet intervened to supersede the common law, to superintend those offences which are prejudicial to the public welfare. Such occasions will be rare, for Parliament has not been slow to legislate when attention has been sufficiently aroused. But gaps remain and will always remain, since no one can foresee every way in which the wickedness of man may disrupt the order of society. Let me take a single instance . . . Let it be supposed that at some future, perhaps early, date homosexual practices between adult consenting males are no longer a crime. Would it not be an offence if even without obscenity such practices were publicly advocated and encouraged by pamphlet and advertisement? Or must we wait till Parliament finds time to deal with such conduct? I say, my Lords, that if the common law is powerless in such an event then we should no longer do her reverence. But I say that her hand is still powerful and that it is for her Majesty's Judges to play the part which Lord Mansfield pointed out to them.[6]

[6] Shaw v. Director of Public Prosecutions (1961) 2 A.E.R. at pp. 452–53. (1962) A.C. at p. 268.

This is no doubt a fine specimen of English judicial rhetoric in the baroque manner. Later judges may dismiss much of it as *obiter dictum*. But the interpretation given by the House of Lords to the exceedingly vague and indeed obscure idea of corrupting public morals has fashioned a very formidable weapon for punishing immorality as such. For it is clear from the form of direction to the jury which the House of Lords approved in this case that no limits are in practice imposed by the need to establish anything which would be ordinarily thought of as a "conspiracy" or as "corruption." These strong words have, as Lord Reid said, been "watered down," and all that has to be established is that the accused agreed to do or say something which in the opinion of a jury might "lead another morally astray."[7] There need moreover be no approach to the "public" nor need the morality in question be "public" in any sense other than being the generally accepted morality.

Legal writers in England have not yet worked out the relation between this vastly comprehensive common law offence and those statutes which define certain specific offences concerned with sexual morality. But it is certainly arguable that the prosecuting authorities may now avail themselves of this common law offence to avoid the restrictions imposed by statute or statutory defences. Thus the statute[8] under which the publishers of D. H. Lawrence's

[7] (1961) 2 A.E.R. at pp. 461, 466. (1962) A.C. at p. 282.
[8] The Obscene Publications Act 1959.

Lady Chatterley's Lover were unsuccessfully prosecuted in England last year provides that the interests of science, literature, and art or learning shall be taken into consideration, and if it is proved that on these grounds publication is justified as being for the public good, no offence under the statute is committed. Evidence as to these merits was accordingly received in that case. Had the publishers been charged with conspiring to corrupt public morals, the literary or artistic merits of the book would have been irrelevant, and the prosecution might very well have succeeded. In the same way, though Parliament in recent legislation has refrained from making prostitution itself a crime, as distinct from soliciting in a street or public place,[9] it seems that it is open to the Courts under the doctrine of Shaw's case to do what Parliament has not done. Some apprehension that it may be so used has already been expressed.[10]

The importance attached by the judges in Shaw's case to the revival of the idea that the Courts should function as the *custos morum* or "the general censor and guardian of the public manners" may be gauged from two things. The first is that this revival was plainly a deliberate act of policy; for the antique cases relied upon as precedents plainly permitted, even under the rigorous English doc-

[9] The Street Offences Act 1959.
[10] *Manchester Guardian,* January 31, 1962; comment on Weisz v. Monahan (1962) 2 W.L.R. 262. Cf. also R. v. Quinn (1961) 3 W.L.R. 611.

trine of precedent, a decision either way. Secondly, the judges seemed willing to pay a high price in terms of the sacrifice of other values for the establishment—or re-establishment—of the Courts as *custos morum*. The particular value which they sacrificed is the principle of legality which requires criminal offences to be as precisely defined as possible, so that it can be known with reasonable certainty beforehand what acts are criminal and what are not. As a result of Shaw's case, virtually any cooperative conduct is criminal if a jury consider it *ex post facto* to have been immoral. Perhaps the nearest counterpart to this in modern European jurisprudence is the idea to be found in German statutes of the Nazi period that anything is punishable if it is deserving of punishment according "to the fundamental conceptions of a penal law and sound popular feeling."[11] So while Mill would have shuddered at the law laid down in Shaw's case as authorising gross invasions of individual liberty, Bentham[12] would have been horrified at its disregard of the legal values of certainty and its extension of what he termed "ex post facto law."[13]

[11] Act of June 28, 1935.

[12] *Principles of the Civil Code,* Part I, Chapter 17 (I [Bowring ed.] *Works* 326).

[13] Shaw's case has been criticised on these grounds by Glanville Williams, "Conspiring to Corrupt," *The Listener,* August 24, 1961, p. 275; Hall Williams, 24 *Mod. L.R.* 631 (1961): "judicial folly"; D. Seaborne Davies, "The House of Lords and the Criminal Law," *J. Soc. Public Teachers of Law* (1961), p. 105: "an egregious per-

PROSTITUTION AND HOMOSEXUALITY

There are other points of interest in Shaw's case. What after all is it to corrupt *morals* or a *morality*? But I shall defer further consideration of this point in order to outline another issue which in England has recently provoked discussion of the law's enforcement of morality and has stimulated efforts to clarify the principles at stake.

Much dissatisfaction has for long been felt in England with the criminal law relating to both prostitution and homosexuality, and in 1954 the committee well known as the Wolfenden Committee was appointed to consider the state of the law. This committee reported[14] in September 1957 and recommended certain changes in the law on both topics. As to homosexuality they recommended by a majority of 12 to 1 that homosexual practices between consenting adults in private should no longer be a crime; as to prostitution they unanimously recommended that, though it should not itself be made illegal, legislation should be passed "to drive it off the streets" on the ground that public soliciting was an offensive nuisance to ordinary citizens. The government eventually introduced legisla-

---

formance." It was welcomed as "an important contribution to the development of the criminal law" by A. L. Goodhart, 77 *Law. Q.R.* 567 (1961).

[14] Report of the Committee on Homosexual Offences and Prostitution (CMD 247) 1957.

tion[15] to give effect to the Committee's recommendations concerning prostitution but not to that concerning homosexuality, and attempts by private members to introduce legislation modifying the law on this subject have so far failed.

What concerns us here is less the fate of the Wolfenden Committee's recommendations than the principles by which these were supported. These are strikingly similar to those expounded by Mill in his essay *On Liberty*. Thus section 13 of the Committee's Report reads:

> [The] function [of the criminal law], as we see it, is to preserve public order and decency, to protect the citizen from what is offensive or injurious and to provide sufficient safeguards against exploitation or corruption of others, particularly those who are specially vulnerable because they are young, weak in body or mind or inexperienced. . . .

This conception of the positive functions of the criminal law was the Committee's main ground for its recommendation concerning prostitution that legislation should be passed to suppress the offensive public manifestations of prostitution, but not to make prostitution itself illegal. Its recommendation that the law against homosexual practices between consenting adults in private should be relaxed was based on the principle stated simply in section 61 of the Report as follows: "There must remain a realm of private

[15] The Street Offences Act 1959.

14

morality and immorality which is, in brief and crude terms, not the law's business."

It is of some interest that these developments in England have had near counterparts in America. In 1955 the American Law Institute published with its draft Model Penal Code a recommendation that all consensual relations between adults in private should be excluded from the scope of the criminal law. Its grounds were (*inter alia*) that "no harm to the secular interests of the community is involved in atypical sex practice in private between consenting adult partners";[16] and "there is the fundamental question of the protection to which every individual is entitled against state interference in his personal affairs when he is not hurting others."[17] This recommendation had been approved by the Advisory Committee of the Institute but rejected by a majority vote of its Council. The issue was therefore referred to the annual meeting of the Institute at Washington in May 1955, and the recommendation, supported by an eloquent speech of the late Justice Learned Hand, was, after a hot debate, accepted by a majority of 35 to 24.[18]

It is perhaps clear from the foregoing that Mill's principles are still very much alive in the criticism of law, what-

[16] American Law Institute Model Penal Code, Tentative Draft No. 4, p. 277.

[17] *Ibid.*, p. 278.

[18] An account of the debate is given in *Time*, May 30, 1955, p. 13.

ever their theoretical deficiencies may be. But twice in one hundred years they have been challenged by two masters of the Common Law. The first of these was the great Victorian judge and historian of the Criminal Law, James Fitzjames Stephen. His criticism of Mill is to be found in the sombre and impressive book *Liberty, Equality, Fraternity,*[19] which he wrote as a direct reply to Mill's essay *On Liberty.* It is evident from the tone of this book that Stephen thought he had found crushing arguments against Mill and had demonstrated that the law might justifiably enforce morality as such or, as he said, that the law should be "a persecution of the grosser forms of vice."[20] Nearly a century later, on the publication of the Wolfenden Committee's report, Lord Devlin, now a member of the House of Lords and a most distinguished writer on the criminal law, in his essay on *The Enforcement of Morals*[21] took as his target the Report's contention "that there must be a realm of morality and immorality which is not the law's business" and argued in opposition to it that "the suppression of vice is as much the law's business as the suppression of subversive activities."

Though a century divides these two legal writers, the similarity in the general tone and sometimes in the detail of their arguments is very great. I shall devote the re-

[19] 2nd edition, London, 1874.
[20] *Ibid.,* p. 162.
[21] Oxford University Press, 1959.

mainder of these lectures to an examination of them. I do this because, though their arguments are at points confused, they certainly still deserve the compliment of rational opposition. They are not only admirably stocked with concrete examples, but they express the considered views of skilled, sophisticated lawyers experienced in the administration of the criminal law. Views such as theirs are still quite widely held especially by lawyers both in England and in this country; it may indeed be that they are more popular, in both countries, than Mill's doctrine of Liberty.

POSITIVE AND CRITICAL MORALITY

Before we consider the detail of these arguments, it is, I think, necessary to appreciate three different but connected features of the question with which we are concerned.

In all the three formulations given on page 4 it is plain that the question is one *about* morality, but it is important to observe that it is also itself a question *of* morality. It is the question whether the enforcement of morality is morally justified; so morality enters into the question in two ways. The importance of this feature of the question is that it would plainly be no sufficient answer to show that in fact in some society—our own or others—it was widely regarded as morally quite right and proper to enforce, by legal punishment, compliance with the accepted morality. No one who seriously debates this question would regard Mill as refuted by the simple demonstration that there are some societies in which the generally shared morality endorses its own enforcement by law, and does so even in those cases where the immorality was thought harmless to others. The existence of societies which condemn association between white and coloured persons as immoral and punish it by law still leaves our question to be argued. It is true that Mill's critics have often made much of the fact that English law does in several instances, apparently with the support of popular morality, punish immorality as such, especially in sexual matters; but they have usually admitted that this is where the argument begins, not where it ends. I shall indeed later claim that the play made by some legal writers with what they treat as examples of the legal enforcement of morality "as such" is sometimes confused. But they do not, at any rate, put forward their case as simply proved by pointing to these social facts. Instead they attempt to base their own conclusion that it is morally justifiable to use the criminal law in this way on principles which they believe to be universally applicable, and which they think are either quite obviously rational or will be seen to be so after discussion.

Thus Lord Devlin bases his affirmative answer to the question on the quite general principle that it is permissible for any society to take the steps needed to preserve its own existence as an organized society,[22] and he thinks that immorality—even private sexual immorality—may, like treason, be something which jeopardizes a society's existence. Of course many of us may doubt this general principle, and not merely the suggested analogy with treason. We might wish to argue that whether or not a society is justified in taking steps to preserve itself must depend both on what sort of society it is and what the steps to be taken are. If a society were mainly devoted to the cruel persecution of a racial or religious minority, or if the steps to be taken included hideous tortures, it is arguable that what Lord Devlin terms the "disintegration"[23] of such a society would be morally better than its continued existence, and steps ought not to be taken to preserve it. Nonetheless Lord Devlin's principle that a society may take the steps required to preserve its organized existence is not itself tendered as an item of English popular morality, deriving its cogency from its status as part of our institutions. He puts it forward as a principle, rationally acceptable, to be used in the evaluation or criticism of social institutions generally. And it is surely clear that anyone who holds the question whether a society has the "right" to enforce morality, or whether it is morally permissible for any society to enforce its morality by law, to be discussable at all, must be prepared to deploy some such general principles of critical

[22] *The Enforcement of Morals,* pp. 13–14.
[23] *Ibid.,* pp. 14–15.

morality.[24] In asking the question, we are assuming the legitimacy of a standpoint which permits criticism of the institutions of any society, in the light of general principles and knowledge of the facts.

To make this point clear, I would revive the terminology much favoured by the Utilitarians of the last century, which distinguished "positive morality," the morality actually accepted and shared by a given social group, from the general moral principles used in the criticism of actual social institutions including positive morality. We may call such general principles "critical morality" and say that our question is one of critical morality about the legal enforcement of positive morality.

A second feature of our question worth attention is simply that it is a question of *justification*. In asking it we are committed at least to the general critical principle that the use of legal coercion by any society calls for justification as something *prima facie* objectionable to be tolerated only for the sake of some countervailing good. For where there is no *prima facie* objection, wrong, or evil, men do not ask for or give *justifications* of social practices, though they

[24] Lord Devlin has been criticised for asking the question whether society has a *right* to enforce its judgment in matters of morality on the ground that to talk of "right" in such a context is meaningless. See Graham Hughes, "Morals and the Criminal Law," 71 *Yale L.J.* (1962) at 672. This criticism is mistaken, just because Lord Devlin invokes some general critical principle in support of his affirmative answer to the question.

may ask for and give *explanations* of these practices or may attempt to demonstrate their value.

It is salutary to inquire precisely what it is that is *prima facie* objectionable in the legal enforcement of morality; for the idea of legal enforcement is in fact less simple than is often assumed. It has two different but related aspects. One is the actual punishment of the offender. This characteristically involves depriving him of liberty of movement or of property or of association with family or friends, or the infliction upon him of physical pain or even death. All these are things which are assumed to be wrong to inflict on others without special justification, and in fact they are so regarded by the law and morality of all developed societies. To put it as a lawyer would, these are things which, if they are not justified as sanctions, are delicts or wrongs.

The second aspect of legal enforcement bears on those who may never offend against the law, but are coerced into obedience by the threat of legal punishment. This rather than physical restrictions is what is normally meant in the discussion of political arrangements by restrictions on liberty. Such restrictions, it is to be noted, may be thought of as calling for justification for several quite distinct reasons. The unimpeded exercise by individuals of free choice may be held a value in itself with which it is *prima facie* wrong to interfere; or it may be thought valuable because it enables individuals to experiment—even with living—and to discover things valuable both to themselves and to others. But interference with individual liberty may be thought an evil requiring justification for simpler, utilitarian reasons; for it is itself the infliction of a special form of suffering—often very acute—on those whose desires are frustrated by the fear of punishment. This is of particular importance in the case of laws enforcing a sexual morality. They may create misery of a quite special degree. For both the difficulties involved in the repression of sexual impulses and the consequences of repression are quite different from those involved in the abstention from "ordinary" crime. Unlike sexual impulses, the impulse to steal or to wound or even kill is not, except in a minority of mentally abnormal cases, a recurrent and insistent part of daily life. Resistance to the temptation to commit these crimes is not often, as the suppression of sexual impulses generally is, something which affects the development or balance of the individual's emotional life, happiness, and personality.

Thirdly, the distinction already made, between positive morality and principles of critical morality, may serve to dissipate a certain misunderstanding of the question and to clarify its central point. It is sometimes said that the question is not whether it is morally justifiable to enforce morality as such, but only *which* morality may be enforced. Is it only a utilitarian morality condemning activities which are harmful to others? Or is it a morality which also condemns certain activities whether they are harmful or not? This way of regarding the question misrepresents the character of, at any rate, modern controversy. A utilitarian who insists that the law should only punish activities which are harmful adopts this as a critical principle, and, in so doing, he is quite unconcerned with the question whether a utilitarian morality is or is not already accepted as the positive morality of the society to which he applies his critical principles. If it is so accepted, that is not, in his view, the reason why it should be enforced. It is true that if he is successful in preaching his message to a given society, members of it will then be compelled to behave as utilitarians in certain ways, but these facts do not mean that the vital difference between him and his opponent is only as to the content of the morality to be enforced. For as may be seen from the main criticisms of Mill, the Utilitarian's opponent, who insists that it is morally permissible to enforce morality as such, believes that the mere fact that certain rules or standards of behaviour enjoy the status of a society's positive morality is the reason—or at least part of the reason—which justifies their enforcement by law. No doubt in older controversies the opposed positions were different: the question may have been whether the state could punish only activities causing secular harm or also acts of disobedience to what were believed to be divine commands or prescriptions of Natural Law. But what is crucial to the dispute in its modern form is the significance to be attached to the historical fact that certain conduct, no matter what, is prohibited by a positive morality. The utilitarian denies that this has any significance sufficient to justify its enforcement; his opponent asserts that it has. These are divergent critical principles which do not differ merely over the content of the morality to be enforced, but over a more fundamental and, surely, more interesting issue.

II

Both in England and in America the criminal law still contains rules which can only be explained as attempts to enforce morality as such: to suppress practices condemned as immoral by positive morality though they involve nothing that would ordinarily be thought of as harm to other persons. Most of the examples come from the sphere of sexual morals, and in England they include laws against various forms of homosexual behaviour between males, sodomy between persons of different sex even if married, bestiality, incest, living on the earnings of prostitution, keeping a house for prostitution, and also, since the decision in Shaw's case, a conspiracy to corrupt public morals, interpreted to mean, in substance, leading others (in the opinion of a jury) "morally astray." To this list some would add further cases: the laws against abortion, against those forms of bigamy or polygamy which do not involve deception, against suicide and the practice of euthanasia.

But, as I shall later argue, the treatment of some of these latter as attempts to enforce morality as such, is a mistake due to the neglect of certain important distinctions.

In America a glance at the penal statutes of the various states of the Union reveals something quite astonishing to English eyes. For in addition to such offences as are punishable under English law, there seems to be no sexual practice, except "normal" relations between husband and wife and solitary acts of masturbation, which is not forbidden by the law of some state. In a very large number of states adultery, which has not been criminally punishable in England since Cromwell's time, is a crime, though, in a minority of states, this is so only if it is open, notorious, or continuous. Fornication is not a criminal offence in England or in most countries of the civilized world, but only a minority of American states do not have statutes making fornication under certain conditions punishable, and some states make even a single act punishable.[1] Besides these statutory provisions there is an unknown quantity of local or municipal enactments which, in some cases, are more restrictive than the state laws, and though these are for that reason of doubtful validity, they have been enforced. In California the penal code does not make prostitution or fornication a crime, yet for many years

[1] See, for a short summary, the American Law Institute, Model Penal Code, Tentative Draft No. 4, pp. 204–10.

persons have been convicted in Los Angeles under a local ordinance of the offence commonly known as "resorting," solely on proof that they used a room for fornication.[2]

No doubt much, and perhaps most, of this American legislation against sexual immorality is as dead a letter as it is commonly said to be. But the facts as to law enforcement are at present very hard to establish. In many states, California among them, the annual criminal statistics do not usually break down figures for sex crimes further than the two heads of "Rape" and "Other sexual offences." But in Boston as late as 1954 the sex laws were reported to receive "normal" enforcement, and in 1948 there were 248 arrests for adultery in that city.[3] No one, I think, should contemplate this situation with complacency, for in combination with inadequate published statistics the existence of criminal laws which are generally not enforced places formidable discriminatory powers in the hands of the police and prosecuting authorities.

Mill's critics have always pointed to the actual existence of laws punishing mere immorality as if this in some way threw doubt on his claim that the criminal law should not

[2] The State Supreme Court in December 1961 held the ordinance to be in conflict with the state laws and void. See in re *Carol Lane,* Crim. No. 6929, 57 A.C. 103, 18 *Cal. Rptr.* 33. This was confirmed after a rehearing on June 28, 1962. 22 *Cal. Rptr.* 857.

[3] American Law Institute, Model Penal Code, Tentative Draft No. 4, p. 205, n. 16.

be used for this purpose. His defenders have indeed complained that the critics were here guilty of fallacious reasoning or irrelevance. John Morley, for example, in a vivid phrase said that in Stephen's book "a good deal of bustling ponderosity is devoted" to establishing the existence of laws of this sort; he thought that Stephen had simply failed to see that "the actual existence of laws of any given kind is wholly irrelevant to Mr. Mill's contention, which is that it would be better if laws of such a kind did not exist."[4] In fact, neither Stephen (except in one place[5]) nor Lord Devlin, who also appeals to the actual content of English criminal law, is guilty of this form of the fallacy of arguing from what is to what should be, nor are they guilty of irrelevance. Stephen, when forced by Morley to state why he regarded his examples as relevant to the argument, explained that he thought it "not irrelevant to show that Mill was at issue with the practical conclusions to which most nations had been led by experience." In somewhat similar fashion Lord Devlin said:

> Is the argument consistent or inconsistent with the fundamental principles of English law as it exists today? That is the first way of testing it though by no means a conclusive one. In the field of jurisprudence one is at liberty to overturn even fundamental conceptions if they are theoretically unsound. But to see how the

[4] Quoted in *Liberty, Equality, Fraternity,* p. 166 n.
[5] *Ibid.,* pp. 171–72.

argument fares under the existing law is a good starting point.[6]

Both writers, I think, in these perhaps not very perspicuous remarks, intend to invoke only the innocuous conservative principle that there is a presumption that common and long established institutions are likely to have merits not apparent to the rationalist philosopher. Nonetheless, when we examine some of the particular rules or principles of criminal law discussed at length by these writers, it is apparent that the use made of them is both confused and confusing. These examples are not drawn from the area of sexual morals, and certainly many, who would wish to align themselves with Mill and protest against the use of the criminal law to punish practices simply because they offend positive morality, might hesitate or refuse to jettison the particular rules of criminal law instanced by these writers. So if they are correctly classed as rules which can only be explained as designed to enforce morality their persuasive force is very considerable. We may indeed, to use Stephen's words, "be disposed to doubt" whether a principle that would condemn these particular rules could be right. But there are, I think, good reasons for disputing these writers' treatment of these rules as examples of the use of the law solely to enforce morality. We are not forced to choose between jettisoning them or assenting to

[6] *The Enforcement of Morals*, p. 7.

the principle that the criminal law may be used for that purpose. Some closer analysis than these authors give to these examples is, however, required, and to this I now turn.

PATERNALISM AND THE ENFORCEMENT OF MORALITY

I shall start with an example stressed by Lord Devlin. He points out[7] that, subject to certain exceptions such as rape, the criminal law has never admitted the consent of the victim as a defence. It is not a defence to a charge of murder or a deliberate assault, and this is why euthanasia or mercy killing terminating a man's life at his own request is still murder. This is a rule of criminal law which many now would wish to retain, though they would also wish to object to the legal punishment of offences against positive morality which harm no one. Lord Devlin thinks that these attitudes are inconsistent, for he asserts of the rule under discussion, "There is only one explanation," and this is that "there are certain standards of behaviour or moral principles which society requires to be observed."[8] Among these are the sanctity of human life and presumably (since the rule applies to assaults) the physical integrity of the person. So in the case of this rule and a number of others Lord Devlin claims that the "function" of the crimi-

[7] *The Enforcement of Morals*, p. 8.   [8] *Ibid.*

nal law is "to enforce a moral principle and nothing else."[9]

But this argument is not really cogent, for Lord Devlin's statement that "there is only one explanation" is simply not true. The rules excluding the victim's consent as a defence to charges of murder or assault may perfectly well be explained as a piece of paternalism, designed to protect individuals against themselves. Mill no doubt might have protested against a paternalistic policy of using the law to protect even a consenting victim from bodily harm nearly as much as he protested against laws used merely to enforce positive morality; but this does not mean that these two policies are identical. Indeed, Mill himself was very well aware of the difference between them: for in condemning interference with individual liberty except to prevent harm to others he mentions *separate* types of inadequate ground which have been proffered for the use of compulsion. He distinguishes "because it will be better for him" and "because it will make him happier" from "because in the opinion of others it would be right."[10]

Lord Devlin says of the attitude of the criminal law to the victim's consent that if the law existed for the protection of the individual there would be no reason why he should avail himself of it if he did not want it.[11] But paternalism —the protection of people against themselves—is a per-

[9] *Ibid.*, p. 9.
[10] *On Liberty*, Chapter 1.
[11] *The Enforcement of Morals*, p. 8.

fectly coherent policy. Indeed, it seems very strange in mid-twentieth century to insist upon this, for the wane of laissez faire since Mill's day is one of the commonplaces of social history, and instances of paternalism now abound in our law, criminal and civil. The supply of drugs or narcotics, even to adults, except under medical prescription is punishable by the criminal law, and it would seem very dogmatic to say of the law creating this offence that "there is only one explanation," namely, that the law was concerned not with the protection of the would-be purchasers against themselves, but only with the punishment of the seller for his immorality. If, as seems obvious, paternalism is a possible explanation of such laws, it is also possible in the case of the rule excluding the consent of the victim as a defence to a charge of assault. In neither case are we forced to conclude with Lord Devlin that the law's "function" is "to enforce a moral principle and nothing else."[12]

In Chapter 5 of his essay Mill carried his protests against paternalism to lengths that may now appear to us fantastic. He cites the example of restrictions of the sale of drugs, and criticises them as interferences with the liberty of the would-be purchaser rather than with that of the seller. No doubt if we no longer sympathise with this criticism this is due, in part, to a general decline in the belief that individuals know their own interests best, and to an

[12] See, for other possible explanations of these rules, Hughes, "Morals and the Criminal Law," p. 670.

increased awareness of a great range of factors which diminish the significance to be attached to an apparently free choice or to consent. Choices may be made or consent given without adequate reflection or appreciation of the consequences; or in pursuit of merely transitory desires; or in various predicaments when the judgment is likely to be clouded; or under inner psychological compulsion; or under pressure by others of a kind too subtle to be susceptible of proof in a law court. Underlying Mill's extreme fear of paternalism there perhaps is a conception of what a normal human being is like which now seems not to correspond to the facts. Mill, in fact, endows him with too much of the psychology of a middle-aged man whose desires are relatively fixed, not liable to be artificially stimulated by external influences; who knows what he wants and what gives him satisfaction or happiness; and who pursues these things when he can.

Certainly a modification in Mill's principles is required, if they are to accommodate the rule of criminal law under discussion or other instances of paternalism. But the modified principles would not abandon the objection to the use of the criminal law merely to enforce positive morality. They would only have to provide that harming others is something we may still seek to prevent by use of the criminal law, even when the victims consent to or assist in the acts which are harmful to them. The neglect of the distinction between paternalism and what I have termed legal

33

moralism is important as a form of a more general error. It is too often assumed that if a law is not designed to protect one man from another its only rationale can be that it is designed to punish moral wickedness or, in Lord Devlin's words, "to enforce a moral principle." Thus it is often urged that statutes punishing cruelty to animals can only be explained in that way. But it is certainly intelligible, both as an account of the original motives inspiring such legislation and as the specification of an aim widely held to be worth pursuing, to say that the law is here concerned with the *suffering,* albeit only of animals, rather than with the immorality of torturing them.[13] Certainly no one who supports this use of the criminal law is thereby bound in consistency to admit that the law may punish forms of immorality which involve no suffering to any sentient being.

THE MORAL GRADATION OF PUNISHMENT

I now turn back to a very different and perhaps more illuminating error made by Stephen, in his effort to show that the criminal law not only should be but actually was a "persecution of the grosser forms of vice,"[14] and not merely an instrument for the prevention of suffering or

[13] Lord Devlin seems quite unaccountably to ignore this point in his brief reference to cruelty to animals, *The Enforcement of Morals,* p. 17.

[14] *Liberty, Equality, Fraternity,* p. 162.

harm. He claimed that certain principles "universally admitted and acted upon as regulating the amount of punishment"[15] showed this to be the case. His argument is simply this. When the question is how severely an offender should be punished, an estimate of the degree of moral wickedness involved in the crime is always relevant. This is why the strength of temptation, diminishing the moral guilt, in most cases operates in mitigation of punishment; whereas if the object of legal punishment were simply to prevent harmful acts this would not be so.

> A judge has before him two criminals, one of whom appears from the circumstances of the case to be ignorant and depraved, and to have given way to a very strong temptation under the influence of the other, who is a man of rank and education, and who committed the offence of which both are convicted under comparatively slight temptation. I will venture to say that if he made any difference between them at all every judge on the English bench would give the first man a lighter sentence than the second.[16]

There is, of course, little doubt that Stephen here accurately portrays conventional views, frequently applied by Courts in administering the criminal law, though perhaps with less agreement now than when Stephen wrote. Certainly many who would protest against the legal enforcement of sexual morality might yet admit or even insist that

[15] *Ibid.*   [16] *Ibid.*, p. 163.

35

greater wickedness should aggravate, and lesser wickedness should mitigate, the severity of punishment. But from
this fact Stephen, like many others, inferred too much. He
claimed that if we attach importance to the principle that
the moral difference between offences should be reflected
in the gradation of legal punishments, this showed that the
object of such punishment was not merely to prevent acts
"dangerous to society" but "to be a persecution of the
grosser forms of vice."[17] And if the object of the criminal
law is (or includes) "promoting virtue" and "preventing
vice,"[18] it follows, he thought, that "it ought to put a restraint upon vice not to such an extent merely as is necessary for definite self-protection but generally on the ground
that vice is a bad thing."[19] So we may make punishable by
law actions which are condemned by society as immoral,
even if they are not harmful.

Surely this argument is a *non sequitur* generated by
Stephen's failure to see that the questions "What sort of
conduct may justifiably be punished?" and "How severely
should we punish different offenses?" are distinct and in-
dependent questions. There are many reasons why we
might wish the legal gradation of the seriousness of crimes,
expressed in its scale of punishments, not to conflict with
common estimates of their comparative wickedness. One
reason is that such a conflict is undesirable on simple utili-

[17] *Liberty, Equality, Fraternity*, p. 162.
[18] *Ibid.*, p. 159.   [19] *Ibid.*, pp. 147–48.

tarian grounds: it might either confuse moral judgments or bring the law into disrepute, or both. Another reason is that principles of justice or fairness between different offenders require morally distinguishable offences to be treated differently and morally similar offences to be treated alike. These principles are still widely respected, although it is also true that there is a growing disinclination to insist on their application where this conflicts with the forward-looking aims of punishment, such as prevention or reform. But those who concede that we should attempt to adjust the severity of punishment to the moral gravity of offences are not thereby committed to the view that punishment merely for immorality is justified. For they can in perfect consistency insist on the one hand that the only justification for having a *system* of punishment is to prevent harm and only harmful conduct should be punished, and, on the other, agree that when the question of the *quantum* of punishment for such conduct is raised, we should defer to principles which make relative moral wickedness of different offenders a partial determinant of the severity of punishment.

It is in general true that we cannot infer from principles applied in deciding the severity of punishment what the aims of the system of punishment are or what sorts of conduct may justifiably be punished. For some of these principles, e.g., the exclusion of torture or cruel punishments, may represent other values with which we may wish to compromise, and our compromise with them may restrict the extent to which we pursue the main values which justify punishment. So if in the course of punishing only harmful activities we think it right (for either of the two reasons distinguished above) to mark moral differences between different offenders, this does not show that we must also think it right to punish activities which are not harmful. It only shows that, in the theory of punishment, what is in the end morally tolerable is apt to be more complex than our theories initially suggest. We cannot usually in social life pursue a single value or a single moral aim, untroubled by the need to compromise with others.

PRIVATE IMMORALITY AND PUBLIC INDECENCY

So far, scrutiny of two examples used by the writers we have considered has established two important distinctions: the distinction between paternalism and the enforcement of morality, and that between justifying the practice of punishment and justifying its amount. Our third example is the crime of bigamy. This is not discussed by Stephen or Lord Devlin, but the punishment of polygamy is cited as an example of the legal enforcement of morality by Dean Rostow in his essay defending Lord Devlin against his critics.[20] It is, however, a curiously complex case, and an

[20] "The Enforcement of Morals," 174 *Cambridge L.J.* (1960) at p. 190. Dean Rostow mainly discusses polygamy "based on sincere

examination of it shows that punishment of bigamy is not to be classed unambiguously as an attempt to enforce morality. In the short discussion of it which follows I shall attempt to show that in this case, as in the two already discussed, those who would wish to retain this rule of criminal law are not thereby committed to the policy of punishing immorality as such; for its punishment can be supported on other reasonable grounds.

In most common law jurisdictions it is a criminal offence for a married person during the lifetime of an existing husband or wife to go through a ceremony of marriage with another person, even if the other person knows of the existing marriage. The punishment of bigamy not involving deception is curious in the following respect. In England and in many other jurisdictions where it is punishable, the sexual cohabitation of the parties is not a criminal offence. If a married man cares to cohabit with another woman—or even several other women—he may do so with impunity so far as the criminal law is concerned. He may set up house and pretend that he is married: he may celebrate his union with champagne and a distribution of wedding cake and with all the usual social ceremonial of a

---

religious belief" rather than "bigamy contracted for pleasure." He asks (rhetorically) "Should we not conclude that monogamy is so fundamental a theme in the existing common morality of the United States that the condemnation of polygamy as a crime is justified even though the law rests on 'feeling' and not on 'reason'?"

valid marriage. None of this is illegal; but if he goes through a ceremony of marriage, the law steps in not merely to declare it invalid but to punish the bigamist.

Why does the law interfere at this point, leaving the substantial immorality of sexual cohabitation alone? Various answers have been given to this question. Some have suggested that the purpose of the legal punishment of bigamy is to protect public records from confusion, or to frustrate schemes to misrepresent illegitimate children as legitimate. The American Law Institute suggests in its commentary on the draft Model Penal Code that bigamous adultery, even where it does not involve deception, might call for punishment because it is a public affront and provocation to the first spouse, and also because cohabitation under the colour of matrimony is specially likely "to result in desertion, non-support, and divorce."[21] These, it is urged, are harms to individuals which the criminal law may properly seek to prevent by punishment.

Some at least of these suggested grounds seem more ingenious than convincing. The harms they stress may be real enough; yet many may still think that a case for punishing bigamy would remain even if these harms were unlikely to result, or if they were catered for by the creation of specific offences which penalized not the bigamy but, for example, the causing of false statements to be entered into official records. Perhaps most who find these various justi-

[21] See p. 220.

fications of the existing law unconvincing but still wish to retain it would urge that in a country where deep religious significance is attached to monogamous marriage and to the act of solemnizing it, the law against bigamy should be accepted as an attempt to protect religious feelings from offence by a public act desecrating the ceremony. Again as with the two previous examples, the question is whether those who think that the use of the criminal law for these purposes is in principle justified are inconsistent if they also deny that the law may be used to punish immorality as such.

I do not think that there is any inconsistency in this combination of attitudes, but there is a need for one more important distinction. It is important to see that if, in the case of bigamy, the law intervenes in order to protect religious sensibilities from outrage by a public act, the bigamist is punished neither as irreligious nor as immoral but as a nuisance. For the law is then concerned with the offensiveness to others of his public conduct, not with the immorality of his private conduct, which, in most countries, it leaves altogether unpunished. In this case, as in the case of ordinary crimes which cause physical harm, the protection of those likely to be affected is certainly an intelligible aim for the law to pursue, and it certainly could not be said of this case that "the function of the criminal law is to enforce a moral principle and nothing else." It is to be noted that Lord Devlin himself, unlike his defender Dean

Rostow, seems to attend to this distinction; for he does not include bigamy in his list of crimes which the principles of the Wolfenden Report would compel us to reject. This is not an oversight, for he specifically says of those which are included in the list that "they are all acts which can be done in private and without offence to others."[22]

It is perhaps doubtful whether Mill's principles as stated in the essay *On Liberty* would have allowed the punishment of bigamy, where no deception was involved, on the ground that it was a public act offensive to religious feelings. For although it is clear that he thought consideration might be due to the "feelings" as well as to the "interests" of others, and an act causing offence to feelings might deserve at least moral blame, he both asserts this and qualifies it in language which is notoriously very difficult to interpret. He seems to have thought that blame and punishment for offence to feelings were justified only if at least two conditions were satisfied: first that some close association or special relationship existed between the parties making consideration an obligation to "assignable" individuals; and secondly that the harm should not be "merely contingent" or "constructive."[23]

---

[22] *The Enforcement of Morals*, p. 9. Nonetheless Lord Devlin warmly endorses Dean Rostow's defence. See "Law, Democracy, and Morality," 110 *University of Pennsylvania L.R.* (1962) at p. 640.

[23] *On Liberty*, Chapter 4.

If we disregard the first of these conditions as too restrictive, and interpret the second to mean only that the offence to feelings should be both serious and likely, the question whether or not to punish bigamy will depend on comparative estimates (over which men may of course differ) of the seriousness of the offence to feelings and of the sacrifice of freedom and suffering demanded and imposed by the law. Supporters of the law could certainly argue that very little sacrifice or suffering is demanded by the law in this instance. It denies only one, though doubtless the most persuasive, item of the appearance of legal respectability to parties who are allowed to enjoy the substance and parade all the other simulacra of a valid marriage. The case is therefore utterly different from attempts to enforce sexual morality which may demand the repression of powerful instincts with which personal happiness is intimately connected. On the other hand, opponents of the law may plausibly urge, in an age of waning faith, that the religious sentiments likely to be offended by the public celebration of a bigamous marriage are no longer very widespread or very deep and it is enough that such marriages are held legally invalid.

The example of bigamy shows the need to distinguish between the immorality of a practice and its aspect as a public offensive act or nuisance. This is of general importance; for English law has often in the course of its development come to view in just this light conduct previously punished simply because it was forbidden by accepted religion or morality. Thus any denial of the truths of the Christian religion was once punished in England as blasphemy, whereas now it is only punishable if it is made in an offensive or insulting manner, likely to cause a breach of the peace. Those who support this modern form of the punishment of blasphemy are not, of course, committed to belief in the religion of those whose feelings are thereby protected from insult. They may indeed quite consistently oppose any attempt to enforce conformity with that or any religion.

In sexual matters a similar line generally divides the punishment of immorality from the punishment of indecency. The Romans distinguished the province of the Censor, concerned with morals, from that of the Aedile, concerned with public decency, but in modern times perhaps insufficient attention has been given to this distinction.[24] Indeed, Lord Simonds in his speech in the House of Lords in Shaw's case went out of his way to profess indifference to it.

> It matters little what label is given to the offending act. To one of your Lordships it may appear an affront to public decency, to another considering that it may succeed in its obvious intention of provoking libidinous desires it will seem a corruption of morality.[25]

[24] But see "The Censor as Aedile," *Times Literary Suppl.*, August 4, 1961.

[25] (1961) 2 A.E.R. at 452.

But the distinction is in fact both clear and important. Sexual intercourse between husband and wife is not immoral, but if it takes place in public it is an affront to public decency. Homosexual intercourse between consenting adults in private is immoral according to conventional morality, but not an affront to public decency, though it would be both if it took place in public. But the fact that the same act, if done in public, could be regarded both as immoral and as an affront to public decency must not blind us to the difference between these two aspects of conduct and to the different principles on which the justification of their punishment must rest. The recent English law relating to prostitution attends to this difference. It has not made prostitution a crime but punishes its public manifestation in order to protect the ordinary citizen, who is an unwilling witness of it in the streets, from something offensive.

It may no doubt be objected that too much has been made in this discussion of the distinction between what is done in public and what is done in private. For offence to feelings, it may be said, is given not only when immoral activities or their commercial preliminaries are thrust upon unwilling eyewitnesses, but also when those who strongly condemn certain sexual practices as immoral learn that others indulge in them in private. Because this is so, it is pointless to attend to the distinction between what is done privately and what is done in public; and if we do not attend to it, then the policies of punishing men for mere immorality and punishing them for conduct offensive to the feelings of others, though conceptually distinct, would not differ in practice. All conduct strongly condemned as immoral would then be punishable.

It is important not to confuse this argument with the thesis, which I shall later examine, that the preservation of an existing social morality is itself a value justifying the use of coercion. The present argument invokes in support of the legal enforcement of morality not the values of morality but Mill's own principle that coercion may be justifiably used to prevent harm to others. Various objections may be made to this use of the principle. It may be said that the distress occasioned by the bare thought that others are offending in private against morality cannot constitute "harm," except in a few neurotic or hypersensitive persons who are literally "made ill" by this thought. Others may admit that such distress is harm, even in the case of normal persons, but argue that it is too slight to outweigh the great misery caused by the legal enforcement of sexual morality.

Although these objections are not without force, they are of subsidiary importance. The fundamental objection surely is that a right to be protected from the distress which is inseparable from the bare knowledge that others are acting in ways you think wrong, cannot be acknowledged by anyone who recognises individual liberty as a value.

For the extension of the utilitarian principle that coercion may be used to protect men from harm, so as to include their protection from this form of distress, cannot stop there. If distress incident to the belief that others are doing wrong is harm, so also is the distress incident to the belief that others are doing what you do not want them to do. To punish people for causing this form of distress would be tantamount to punishing them simply because others object to what they do; and the only liberty that could coexist with this extension of the utilitarian principle is liberty to do those things to which no one seriously objects. Such liberty plainly is quite nugatory. Recognition of individual liberty as a value involves, as a minimum, acceptance of the principle that the individual may do what he wants, even if others are distressed when they learn what it is that he does—unless, of course, there are other good grounds for forbidding it. No social order which accords to individual liberty any value could also accord the right to be protected from distress thus occasioned.

Protection from shock or offence to feelings caused by some public display is, as most legal systems recognise, another matter. The distinction may sometimes be a fine one. It is so, in those cases such as the desecration of venerated objects or ceremonies where there would be no shock or offence to feeling, if those on whom the public display is obtruded had not subscribed to certain religious or moral beliefs. Nonetheless the use of punishment to protect those made vulnerable to the public display by their own beliefs leaves the offender at liberty to do the same thing in private, if he can. It is not tantamount to punishing men simply because others object to what they do.

THE MODERATE AND THE EXTREME THESIS

When we turn from these examples which are certainly disputable to the positive grounds held to justify the legal enforcement of morality it is important to distinguish a moderate and an extreme thesis, though critics of Mill have sometimes moved from one to the other without marking the transition. Lord Devlin seems to me to maintain, for most of his essay, the moderate thesis and Stephen the extreme one.

According to the moderate thesis, a shared morality is the cement of society; without it there would be aggregates of individuals but no society. "A recognized morality" is, in Lord Devlin's words, "as necessary to society's existence as a recognized government,"[26] and though a particular act of immorality may not harm or endanger or corrupt others nor, when done in private, either shock or give offence to others, this does not conclude the matter. For we must not view conduct in isolation from its effect on the moral code: if we remember this, we can see that one who is "no menace to others" nonetheless may by his immoral

[26] *The Enforcement of Morals,* p. 13.

conduct "threaten one of the great moral principles on which society is based."[27] In this sense the breach of moral principle is an offence "against society as a whole,"[28] and society may use the law to preserve its morality as it uses it to safeguard anything else essential to its existence. This is why "the suppression of vice is as much the law's business as the suppression of subversive activities."[29]

By contrast, the extreme thesis does not look upon a shared morality as of merely instrumental value analogous to ordered government, and it does not justify the punishment of immorality as a step taken, like the punishment of treason, to preserve society from dissolution or collapse. Instead, the enforcement of morality is regarded as a thing of value, even if immoral acts harm no one directly, or indirectly by weakening the moral cement of society. I do not say that it is possible to allot to one or other of these two theses every argument used, but they do, I think, characterise the main critical positions at the root of most arguments, and they incidentally exhibit an ambiguity in the expression "enforcing morality as such." Perhaps the clearest way of distinguishing the two theses is to see that there are always two levels at which we may ask whether some breach of positive morality is harmful. We may ask first, Does this act harm anyone independently of its repercussion on the shared morality of society? And secondly we may ask, Does this act affect the shared morality and there-

[27] *Ibid.,* p. 8.   [28] *Ibid.*   [29] *Ibid.,* p. 15.

by weaken society? The moderate thesis requires, if the punishment of the act is to be justified, an affirmative answer at least at the second level. The extreme thesis does not require an affirmative answer at either level.

Lord Devlin appears to defend the moderate thesis. I say "appears" because, though he says that society has the right to enforce a morality as such on the ground that a shared morality is essential to society's existence, it is not at all clear that for him the statement that immorality jeopardizes or weakens society is a statement of empirical fact. It seems sometimes to be an *a priori* assumption, and sometimes a necessary truth and a very odd one. The most important indication that this is so is that, apart from one vague reference to "history" showing that "the loosening of moral bonds is often the first stage of disintegration,"[30] no evidence is produced to show that deviation from accepted sexual morality, even by adults in private, is something which, like treason, threatens the existence of society. No reputable historian has maintained this thesis, and there is indeed much evidence against it. As a proposition of fact it is entitled to no more respect than the Emperor Justinian's statement that homosexuality was the cause of earthquakes.[31] Lord Devlin's belief in it, and his apparent indifference to the question of evidence, are at points traceable to an undiscussed assumption. This is that all moral-

[30] *The Enforcement of Morals,* pp. 14–15.
[31] *Novels,* 77 Cap. 1 and 141.

ity—sexual morality together with the morality that forbids acts injurious to others such as killing, stealing, and dishonesty—forms a single seamless web, so that those who deviate from any part are likely or perhaps bound to deviate from the whole. It is of course clear (and one of the oldest insights of political theory) that society could not exist without a morality which mirrored and supplemented the law's proscription of conduct injurious to others. But there is again no evidence to support, and much to refute, the theory that those who deviate from conventional sexual morality are in other ways hostile to society.

There seems, however, to be central to Lord Devlin's thought something more interesting, though no more convincing, than the conception of social morality as a seamless web. For he appears to move from the acceptable proposition that *some* shared morality is essential to the existence of any society to the unacceptable proposition that a society is identical[32] with its morality as that is at any given moment of its history, so that a change in its morality is tantamount to the destruction of a society. The former proposition might be even accepted as a necessary rather than an empirical truth depending on a quite plausible definition of society as a body of men who hold certain moral views in common. But the latter proposition is absurd. Taken strictly, it would prevent us saying that the morality of a

[32] See, for this important point, Richard Wollheim, "Crime, Sin, and Mr. Justice Devlin," *Encounter*, November 1959, p. 34.

given society had changed, and would compel us instead to say that one society had disappeared and another one taken its place. But it is only on this absurd criterion of what it is for the same society to continue to exist that it could be asserted without evidence that any deviation from a society's shared morality threatens its existence.

It is clear that only this tacit identification of a society with its shared morality supports Lord Devlin's denial that there could be such a thing as private immorality and his comparison of sexual immorality, even when it takes place "in private," with treason. No doubt it is true that if deviations from conventional sexual morality are tolerated by the law and come to be known, the conventional morality might change in a permissive direction, though this does not seem to be the case with homosexuality in those European countries where it is not punishable by law. But even if the conventional morality did so change, the society in question would not have been destroyed or "subverted." We should compare such a development not to the violent overthrow of government but to a peaceful constitutional change in its form, consistent not only with the preservation of a society but with its advance.

III

In the last lecture I distinguished a moderate and an extreme form of the thesis that the criminal law might justifiably be used to enforce morality. According to the moderate thesis, there is certainly a contrast between crimes obviously harmful to others (such as murder or assault) and mere immoral conduct, forbidden by law, which takes place between consenting adults in private. This contrast seems at first sight to warrant our regarding the legal prohibition and punishment of the latter as the enforcement of morality "as such." Nonetheless, according to this theory, once we grasp the truth that a society's morality is necessary for its very existence, it becomes clear that any immoral act, however private its performance, must in the long run be harmful because "it threatens the moral principles on which society is based" and so jeopardizes society's existence. So on this view the enforcement of morality (which is assumed to be required for its preservation) is necessary for the very existence of society and is justified for that reason.

The extreme thesis has many variants, and it is not always clear which of them its advocates are concerned to urge. According to some variants, the legal enforcement of morality is only of instrumental value: it is merely a means, though an indispensable one, for preserving morality, whereas the preservation of morality is the end, valuable in itself, which justifies its legal enforcement. According to other variants, there is something intrinsically valuable in the legal enforcement of morality. What is common to all varieties of the extreme thesis is that, unlike the moderate thesis, they do not hold the enforcement of morality or its preservation to be valuable merely because of their beneficial consequences in securing the existence of society.

It is to be observed that Lord Devlin hovers somewhat ambiguously between one form of the extreme thesis and the moderate thesis. For if we interpret his crucial statement that the preservation of a society's morality is necessary for its existence as a statement of fact (as the analogy with the suppression of treason suggests we should), then the continued existence of society is something distinguishable from the preservation of its morality. It is, in fact, a desirable consequence of the preservation of its morality, and, on the assumption that the enforcement of morality is identical with or required for its preservation, this desirable consequence justifies the enforcement of morality.

So interpreted, Lord Devlin is an advocate of the moderate thesis and his argument is a utilitarian one. The objection to it is that his crucial statement of fact is unsupported by evidence; it is Utilitarianism without benefit of facts. If, on the other hand, we interpret his statement that any immorality, even in private, threatens the existence of society, not as an empirical statement but as a necessary truth (as the absence of evidence suggests we should), then the continued existence of a society is not something different from the preservation of its morality; it is identical with it. On this view the enforcement of morality is not justified by its valuable consequences in securing society from dissolution or decay. It is justified simply as identical with or required for the preservation of the society's morality. This is a form of the extreme thesis, disguised only by the tacit identification of a society with its morality which I criticised in the last lecture.

Stephen is, I think, a more consistent defender of certain forms of the extreme thesis than Lord Devlin is of the moderate one. But before we consider the argument it is important to recall the complexities contained in the apparently simple notion of the legal enforcement of any kind of conduct. We have already distinguished two aspects of enforcement: the first is that of coercion and consists in securing, by the threat of legal punishment, that people do or abstain from doing what the law enjoins or forbids; the second is that of the actual punishment of those who have broken the law. Besides these forms of enforcement there are others which it is important not to overlook in considering the legal use of "force." Thus steps may be taken which render disobedience to the law impossible or difficult, and so frustrate it rather than punish it. An example of this well known in England is the power given to officials by the Obscene Publications Act of 1857 to seize and destroy obscene publications; and in some jurisdictions the law authorises the physical closing of premises used as brothels. A further distinguishable aspect of legal enforcement is the use of pressure to induce those actually engaged in breaking the law or threatening to do so to desist. The fact that the means of pressure used are also used for punishment should not blind us to the difference. The most common form in England and America of this method of enforcement is the imprisonment, until they submit, of those who refuse to comply with a Court's order, and the "cease and desist orders" under which a daily-mounting fine is imposed as long as disobedience lasts. No doubt the first of these is usually presented as a form of punishment for "contempt of Court." An apology as well as obedience to the Court is usually required to terminate imprisonment for contempt, but its primary use is as a form of pressure available to those interested in securing compliance with the law.

These distinctions are important for present purposes, because the extreme thesis that the legal enforcement of morality is justified not by its consequences but as a value in itself may need separate consideration with regard to different aspects of enforcement. Moreover, reflection on these different aspects will force us to question the assumption, certainly made by Lord Devlin and possibly also by Stephen, that the enforcement of a morality and its preservation are identical or at least necessarily connected.

Enforcement as coercion.—If we consider the first aspect of enforcement, namely, coercion by threats, a very great difference is apparent between inducing persons through fear of punishment to abstain from actions which are harmful to others, and inducing them to abstain from actions which deviate from accepted morality but harm no one. The value attached to the first is easy to understand; for the protection of human beings from murder or violence or others forms of injury remains a good whatever the motives are by which others are induced to abstain from these crimes. But where there is no harm to be prevented and no potential victim to be protected, as is often the case where conventional sexual morality is disregarded, it is difficult to understand the assertion that conformity, even if motivated merely by fear of the law's punishment, is a value worth pursuing, notwithstanding the misery and sacrifice of freedom which it involves. The attribution of value to mere conforming behaviour, in abstraction from both motive and consequences, belongs not to morality but to taboo. This does not mean that we cannot intelligibly attribute value to lives dedicated to ideals of chastity or self-denial. Indeed, the achievement of self-discipline not only in sexual matters but in other fields of conduct must on any theory of morality be a constituent of a good life. But what is valuable here is *voluntary* restraint, not submission to coercion, which seems quite empty of moral value.

It may of course be argued that, though for these reasons legally enforced conformity is of no value in itself, it is yet indispensable as a means of teaching or maintaining a morality which is for the most part practised voluntarily. "The fact that men are hanged for murder is one great reason why murder is considered so dreadful a crime."[1] There is nothing self-contradictory in such theories that the threat of legal punishment is required to create or maintain the voluntary practice of morality. But these are theories requiring the support of empirical facts, and there is very little evidence to support the idea that morality is best taught by fear of legal punishment. Much morality is certainly taught and sustained without it, and where morality is taught with it, there is the standing danger that fear of punishment may remain the sole motive for conformity.

Enforcement as punishment.—The second aspect of legal enforcement consists not in the threat but in the

[1] Report of the Royal Commission on Capital Punishment (CMD 8932) s. 61. The quotation is from Stephen's article on capital punishment in *Fraser's Magazine,* June 1864, p. 761.

actual infliction of punishment on offenders. If we ask what value this can have where the conduct punished is not harmful, the most obvious answer is a retributive "theory" of punishment: the claim that what justifies the infliction of punishment is not that it has beneficial consequences on society or on the person punished, but that pain is morally the appropriate or "fitting" return for moral evil done. I cannot here undertake a full-scale examination of this theory of punishment, but I will draw attention to one salient point. A theory which does not attempt to justify punishment by its results, but simply as something called for by the wickedness of a crime, is certainly most plausible, and perhaps only intelligible, where the crime has harmed others and there is both a wrongdoer and a victim. Even the most faithful adherents of utilitarian doctrine must have felt tempted at times to acknowledge the simple claim that it is right or just that one who has intentionally inflicted suffering on others should himself be made to suffer. I doubt if anyone, reading the records of Auschwitz or Buchenwald, has failed to feel the powerful appeal of this principle; perhaps even the most reflective of those who supported the punishment of the criminals concerned were moved by this principle rather than by the thought that punishment would have beneficial future consequences. But the strength of this form of retribution is surely dependent on there being a victim as well as an offender; for where this is the case, it is possible to conceive of the punishment as a measure designed to prevent the wrongdoer prospering when his victims suffer or have perished. The principles requiring this to be done are certainly analogous to those of justice or fairness in the distribution of happiness and suffering—principles which permeate other areas of morality. I should not myself argue that even this analogy is sufficient. Yet it is certainly something which should prevent our dismissing all retributive theory out of hand. But where there is no victim but only a transgression of a moral rule, the view that punishment is still called for as a proper return for the immorality lacks even this support. Retribution here seems to rest on nothing but the implausible claim that in morality two blacks make a white: that the evil of suffering added to the evil of immorality as its punishment makes a moral good.

RETRIBUTION AND DENUNCIATION

In his chapter on Mill's doctrine of liberty in relation to morals Stephen was principally concerned to identify and expose the inconsistencies and false assumptions about human nature and society by which, as he believed, Mill's arguments were vitiated. He devoted comparatively little space to explaining the positive grounds for his own claim that the criminal law should be used not only for protection "against acts dangerous to society" but as a "persecution of the grosser forms of vice."[2] It is not, indeed, easy to disentangle from his arguments any very precise account of the values which he thought the legal enforcement of morality constituted or secured. The most prominent—and to many the most distasteful—feature of his thought on these matters is his general insistence on the legitimacy or "healthiness"[3] of hatred or resentment for the criminal and the desire for revenge on him. It is easy to conclude from his emphasis on this theme that Stephen relies for his positive case on a simple and indeed crude form of retributive theory: that punishment of the criminal is justified because "the feeling of hatred and the desire of vengeance are important elements in human nature which ought in such cases to be satisfied in a regular public and legal manner."[4]

Stephen's insistence on the legitimacy of hatred and of the wish for revenge is certainly central in his whole outlook on punishment, and later English judges have attached similar importance to them. The former Lord Chief Justice of England, Lord Goddard, in the last debate on capital punishment in the House of Lords, said, "I do not see how it can be either non-Christian or other than praiseworthy that the country should be willing to avenge crime."[5] But it would not be fair to Stephen to

[2] *Liberty, Equality, Fraternity*, p. 162.
[3] *Ibid.*, pp. 162, 165.   [4] *Ibid.*, p. 162.
[5] 198 H.L. Debates (5th Series) 743 (1956).

present this form of retributive theory as the whole of his doctrine; for there is at least one other element woven into his arguments. This I shall call, for reasons which will appear, the denunciatory element. Though Stephen himself does not distinguish this from his own form of retributive theory, it is worth isolating for scrutiny, because it figures largely in the conception of the function and justification of punishment which is even today characteristic of the English judiciary and is shared by many conservative English and American lawyers.

It is important for the understanding of Stephen's views on the legal enforcement of morality to notice that he, like Lord Devlin, assumes that the society to which his doctrine is to apply is marked by a considerable degree of moral solidarity, and is deeply disturbed by infringements of its moral code. Just as for Lord Devlin the morality to be enforced by law must be "public," in the sense that it is generally shared and identifiable by the triple marks of "intolerance, indignation, and disgust,"[6] so for Stephen "you cannot punish anything which public opinion as expressed in the common practice of society does not strenuously and unequivocally condemn . . . To be able to punish a moral majority must be overwhelming."[7] It is possible that in mid-Victorian England these conditions were satisfied in

[6] *The Enforcement of Morals,* p. 17: "They are the forces behind the moral law."

[7] *Liberty, Equality, Fraternity,* pp. 173–74.

relation to "that considerable number of acts" which according to Stephen were treated as crimes merely because they were regarded as grossly immoral. Perhaps an "overwhelming moral majority" then actually did harbour the healthy desire for revenge of which he speaks and which is to be gratified by the punishment of the guilty. But it would be sociologically naïve to assume that these conditions obtain in contemporary England at least as far as sexual morality is concerned. The fact that there is lip service to an official sexual morality should not lead us to neglect the possibility that in sexual, as in other matters, there may be a number of mutually tolerant moralities, and that even where there is some homogeneity of practice and belief, offenders may be viewed not with hatred or resentment but with amused contempt or pity.

In a sense, therefore, Stephen's doctrine, and much of Lord Devlin's, may seem to hover in the air above the *terra firma* of contemporary social reality; it may be a well-articulated construction, interesting because it reveals the outlook characteristic of the English judiciary but lacking application to contemporary society. But with this possibly illusory picture of society in mind, Stephen sometimes writes as if the function of punishment were not so much retributive as denunciatory; not so much to gratify feelings of hatred or revenge as to express in emphatic form moral condemnation of the offender and to "ratify" the morality which he has violated. This idea is present in

Liberty, Equality, Fraternity in a passage where Stephen speaks of the criminal law giving "distinct shape to the feeling of anger" as well as "distinct satisfaction to the desire for vengeance."[8] The same idea is, however, more elaborately and clearly expressed in his *History of the Criminal Law*:

> The sentence of the law is to the moral sentiment of the public in relation to any offence what a seal is to hot wax. It converts into a permanent final judgment what might otherwise be a transient sentiment . . . In short the infliction of punishment by law gives definite expression and solemn ratification and justification to the hatred which is excited by the commission of the offence and which constitutes the moral or popular, as distinct from the conscientious, sanction of that part of morality which is also sanctioned by the criminal law. . . . The forms in which deliberate anger and righteous disapprobation are expressed, and the execution of criminal justice is the most emphatic of such forms, stand to the one set of passions in the same relation which marriage stands to the other [sexual passions].[9]

There is no doubt much that is unclear in this theory; in particular, Stephen speaks mysteriously of the punishment "justifying" the feeling which it expresses. But its general drift is clear, and it is a theme which later judges have

[8] P. 165.
[9] *A History of the Criminal Law of England*, II, 81–82.

echoed. Thus in our own day Lord Denning in his evidence to the Royal Commission on Capital Punishment said:

> The punishment for grave crimes should adequately reflect the revulsion felt by the majority of citizens for them. It is a mistake to consider the object of punishment as being deterrent or reformative or preventive and nothing else. The ultimate justification of any punishment is not that it is a deterrent but that it is the emphatic denunciation by the community of a crime and from this point of view there are some murders which in the present state of opinion demand the most emphatic denunciation of all, namely the death penalty.[10]

Notwithstanding the eminence of its legal advocates, this justification of punishment, especially when applied to conduct not harmful to others, seems to rest on a strange amalgam of ideas. It represents as a value to be pursued at the cost of human suffering the bare expression of moral condemnation, and treats the infliction of suffering as a uniquely appropriate or "emphatic" mode of expression. But is this really intelligible? Is the mere expression of moral condemnation a thing of value in itself to be pursued at this cost? The idea that we may punish offenders against a moral code, not to prevent harm or suffering or even the repetition of the offence but simply as a means of

[10] Report of the Royal Commission on Capital Punishment, s. 53.

venting or emphatically expressing moral condemnation, is uncomfortably close to human sacrifice as an expression of religious worship. But even if we waive this objection another remains to be faced. What is meant by the claim that the punishment of offenders is an appropriate way of expressing emphatic moral condemnation? The normal way in which moral condemnation is expressed is by *words,* and it is not clear, if denunciation is really what is required, why a solemn public statement of disapproval would not be the most "appropriate" or "emphatic" means of expressing this. Why should a denunciation take the form of punishment?

It is, I think, probable that what the advocates of this theory really mean by an "emphatic" denunciation and the "appropriate" expression of moral condemnation is one that is effective in instilling or strengthening in the offender and in others respect for the moral code which has been violated. But then the theory assumes a different character; it is no longer the theory that the legal enforcement of morality is a value apart from its consequences; it becomes the theory that the legal enforcement of morality is valuable because it preserves an existing morality. This is no doubt the most plausible form of the extreme thesis. But unless it is treated, as Stephen at times appears to treat it, as intuitively obvious, to be accepted without argument or appeal to any general principle of critical morality, it is open to a variety of major criticisms.

The first of these criticisms concerns a matter of fact already mentioned: the assertion that legal enforcement does operate in the manner supposed to maintain an existent social morality requires evidence in support, and at least in relation to sexual morality there is little to be found. No doubt the issues here are quite complex: in any full investigation of the part played by legal prohibition in sustaining the conviction that conduct is morally wrong, we should have to distinguish between various types of immorality. Some, like fornication, though they may be quite sincerely condemned morally, represent temptations to a majority of men; others, such as incest or homosexuality, are practices for which most men may feel aversion and disgust. In relation to the latter, it would be very surprising if legal prohibition were a significant factor in preserving the general sense that the practice is immoral. For if there is on these matters what Lord Devlin calls general "intolerance, indignation, and disgust" and Stephen calls "an overwhelming moral majority" (and only where these exist do they think legal punishment of immorality is justifiable), the conviction that such practices are morally wrong is surely inseparable in the mind of the majority from instinctive repulsion and the deep feeling that they are "unnatural." The notion that the overwhelming moral majority would or even could change heart morally and shed these deep instinctive feelings, if the State did not reflect in legal punishment their moral views on homosexuality, seems fantastic and is quite at variance with the experience of those countries where homosexuality between consenting adults in private is not legally punished. Of course this is not to deny that where the law forbids these practices there will be some who abstain from them only from fear of punishment or because, in Stephen's phrase, they respect the law's "solemn ratification" of existent social morals however much it frustrates their own instincts. But their abstention on these grounds contributes nothing to the general sense that these practices are morally wrong.

The real solvent of social morality, as one critic of Lord Devlin has pointed out,[11] is not the failure of the law to endorse its restrictions with legal punishment, but free critical discussion. It is this—or the self-criticism which it engenders—that forces apart mere instinctive disgust from moral condemnation. If in our own day the "overwhelming moral majority" has become divided or hesitant over many issues of sexual morality, the main catalysts have been matters to which the free discussion of sexual morals, in the light of the discoveries of anthropology and psychology, has drawn attention. These matters are very diverse: they include the harmless character of much sexual deviation, the variety of different sexual moralities in different societies, the connection between restrictive sexual morality and harmful repression. Though few now think

[11] Wollheim, "Crime, Sin, and Mr. Justice Devlin," p. 40.

it justifiable to prohibit free discussion on account of its impact on prevalent social morality, Stephen was well aware that his general doctrine committed him to this. He quite frankly stated that he had no objection to it in principle but thought that when he wrote it was no longer practicable.[12]

THE PRESERVATION OF MORALITY
AND MORAL CONSERVATISM

This last consideration brings us to what is really the central issue in the extreme thesis. Let us suppose, contrary to much evidence, that Stephen's picture of society and its moral mechanisms is a realistic one: that there really is a moral code in sexual matters supported by an overwhelming majority and that they are deeply disturbed when it is infringed even by adults in private; that the punishment of offenders really does sustain the sense that the conduct is immoral and without their punishment the prevalent morality would change in a permissive direction. The central question is: Can anything or nothing be said to support the claim that the prevention of this change and the maintenance of the moral *status quo* in a society's morality are values sufficient to offset the cost in human misery which legal enforcement entails? Is it simply a blank

[12] *Liberty, Equality, Fraternity,* Chapter 2, especially pp. 58, 81, 82–84.

assertion, or does it rest on any critical principles connecting what is said to be of value here with other things of value?

Here certain discriminations are needed. There are three propositions concerning the value of preserving social morality which are in perennial danger of confusion. The first of these propositions is the truth that since all social moralities, whatever else they may contain, make provision in some degree for such universal values as individual freedom, safety of life, and protection from deliberately inflicted harm, there will always be much in social morality which is worth preserving even at the cost in terms of these same values which legal enforcement involves. It is perhaps misleading to say with Lord Devlin that social morality, so far as it secures these things, is of value because they are required for the preservation of society; on the contrary, the preservation of any particular society is of value because among other things it secures for human beings some measure of these universal values. It is indeed arguable that a human society in which these values are not recognised at all in its morality is neither an empirical nor a logical possibility, and that even if it were, such a society could be of no practical value for human beings. In conceding this much, however, we must beware of following Lord Devlin in thinking of social morality as a seamless web and of all its provisions as necessary for the existence of the society whose morality it is. We should with Mill be alive to the truth that though these essential universal values must be secured, society can not only survive individual divergences in other fields from its prevalent morality, but profit from them.

Secondly, there is the truth, less familiar and less easy to state in precise terms, that the spirit or attitude of mind which characterises the practice of a social morality is something of very great value and indeed quite vital for men to foster and preserve in any society. For in the practice of any social morality there are necessarily involved what may be called *formal* values as distinct from the *material* values of its particular rules or content. In moral relationships with others the individual sees questions of conduct from an impersonal point of view and applies general rules impartially to himself and to others; he is made aware of and takes account of the wants, expectations, and reactions of others; he exerts self-discipline and control in adapting his conduct to a system of reciprocal claims. These are universal virtues and indeed constitute the specifically moral attitude to conduct. It is true that these virtues are learnt in conforming to the morality of some particular society, but their value is not derived from the fact that they are there accounted virtues. We have only to conduct the Hobbesian experiment of imagining these virtues totally absent to see that they are vital for the conduct of any cooperative form of human life and any successful personal life. No principles of critical morality which paid the least attention to the most elementary facts of human nature and the conditions in which human life has to be led could propose to dispense with them. Hence if by the preservation of morality is meant the preservation of the moral attitude to conduct and its formal values, it is certainly true that it is a value. But, though true, this is really irrelevant to the issue before us; for the preservation of morality in this sense is not identical with and does not require the preservation from change of a society's moral code as it is at any given moment of that society's existence; and *a fortiori* it does not require the legal enforcement of its rules. The moral attitude to conduct has often survived the criticism, the infringement, and the ultimate relaxation of specific moral institutions. The use of legal punishment to freeze into immobility the morality dominant at a particular time in a society's existence may possibly succeed, but even where it does it contributes nothing to the survival of the animating spirit and formal values of social morality and may do much to harm them.

From the preservation of morality in this sense which is so clearly a value we must, then, distinguish mere moral conservatism. This latter amounts to the proposition that the preservation from change of any existent rule of a social morality, whatever its content, is a value and justifies its legal enforcement. This proposition would be at least intelligible if we could ascribe to all social morality the status which theological systems or the doctrine of the Law of Nature ascribes to some fundamental principles. Then, at least, some general principle would have been adduced to support the claim that preservation of any rule of social morality was a value justifying its legal enforcement; something would have been said to indicate the source of this asserted value. The application of these general principles to the case in hand would then be something to be discussed and argued, and moral conservatism would then be a form of critical morality to be used in the criticism of social institutions. It would not then be—as it is when dissociated from all such general principles—a brute dogma, asserting that the preservation of any social morality necessarily outweighs its cost in human misery and deprivation of freedom. In this dogmatic form it in effect withdraws positive morality from the scope of any moral criticism.

No doubt a critical morality based on the theory that all social morality had the status of divine commands or of eternal truth discovered by reason would not for obvious reasons now seem plausible. It is perhaps least plausible in relation to sexual morals, determined as these so obviously are by variable tastes and conventions. Nonetheless, the attempt to defend the legal enforcement of morality on these lines would be something more than the simple unargued assertion that it was justified. It is worth observing that great social theorists like Burke and Hegel, who were among those most anxious to defend the value of the positive morality and customs of particular societies against utilitarian and rationalist critics, never regarded the simple assertion that these were things of value as adequate. Instead they deployed *theories* of human nature and of history in support of their position. Burke's principal argument, expressed in terms of the "wisdom of the ages" and the "finger of providence," is in essence an evolutionary one: the social institutions which have slowly been developed in the course of any society's history represent an accommodation to the needs of that society which is always likely to be more satisfactory to the mass of its members than any ideal scheme of social life which individuals could invent or any legislator could impose. For Hegel the value of the established institutions of any particular society rested on an elaborate metaphysical doctrine, not easily comprehensible and certainly not capable of adequate statement in the single sentence which I devote to it here. In outline, it is the doctrine that the history of human societies is a process by which the Absolute Spirit manifests itself and that each stage in this development is a rational or even a logical step and so a thing of value.

However questionable this background of theory in any particular case may be, it is yet there for rational criticism, acceptance or rejection; it prevents the assertion of the value of social institutions being merely dogmatic. The assertion will stand or fall with the general theories deployed in its support. It should, however, be remembered that an evolutionary defence of tradition and custom such as Burke made against the rationalist revolutionary or critic affords little support for the enforcement by law of social morality. In Burke, perhaps because he was a Whig, however conservative, the value of established institutions resides in the fact that they have developed as the result of the free, though no doubt unconscious, adaptation of men to the conditions of their lives. To use coercion to maintain the moral *status quo* at any point in a society's history would be artificially to arrest the process which gives social institutions their value.

This distinction between the use of coercion to enforce morality and other methods which we in fact use to preserve it, such as argument, advice, and exhortation, is both very important and much neglected in discussions of the present topic. Stephen, in his arguments against Mill,[13] seems most of the time to forget or to ignore these other methods and the great importance which Mill attached to them. For he frequently argues as if Mill's doctrine of liberty meant that men must never express any convictions concerning the conduct of their fellow citizens if that conduct is not harmful to others. It is true that Mill believed that "the state or the public" is not warranted *"for the purposes of repression or punishment"*[14] in deciding that such conduct is good or bad. But it is not true that he thought that concerning such conduct or "the experiments in liv-

[13] *Liberty, Equality, Fraternity*, pp. 126–42.
[14] *Ibid.*, p. 137; *On Liberty*, Chapter 5.

ing" which it represents "no one else has anything to say to it."[15] Nor did he think that society could "draw a line where education ends and perfect moral indifference begins."[16] In making these ill-founded criticisms Stephen not only misunderstood and so misrepresented Mill, but he showed how narrowly he himself conceived of morality and the processes by which it is sustained. For Mill's concern throughout his essay is to restrict the use of coercion, not to promote moral indifference. It is true he includes in the coercion or "constraint" of which he disapproves not only legal enforcement of morality but also other peremptory forms of social pressure such as moral blame and demands for conformity. But it is a disastrous misunderstanding of morality to think that where we cannot use coercion in its support we must be silent and indifferent. In Chapter 4 of his essay Mill takes great pains to show the other resources which we have and should use:

> It would be a great misunderstanding of this doctrine to suppose that it is one of selfish indifference which pretends that human beings have no business with each others conduct in life and that they should not concern themselves about the well-doing or well-being of one another unless their own interest is involved. . . . Human beings owe to each other help to distinguish the better from the worse and encouragement to choose the former and avoid the latter.

[15] *Liberty, Equality, Fraternity*, p. 141.
[16] *Ibid.*, p. 170.

Discussion, advice, argument—all these, since they leave the individual "the final judge," may according to Mill be used in a society where freedom is properly respected. We may even "obtrude" on another "considerations to aid his judgment and exhortations to strengthen his will."[17] We may in extreme cases "warn" him of our adverse judgment or feelings of distaste and contempt. We may avoid his company and caution others against it. Many might think that Mill here comes perilously near to sanctioning coercion even though he regards these things as "strictly inseparable from the unfavourable judgments of others"[18] and never to be inflicted for the sake of punishment. But if he erred in that direction, it is certainly clear that he recognised the important truth that in morality we are not forced to choose between deliberate coercion and indifference.

MORAL POPULISM AND DEMOCRACY

Mill's essay *On Liberty*, like Tocqueville's book *Democracy in America,* was a powerful plea for a clearheaded appreciation of the dangers that accompany the benefits of democratic rule. The greatest of the dangers, in their view, was not that in fact the majority might use their power to oppress a minority, but that, with the spread of democratic ideas, it might come to be thought unobjec-

[17] *On Liberty*, Chapter 4.   [18] *Ibid*.

tionable that they should do so. For Mill, these dangers
were part of the price to be paid for all that is so valuable
in democratic government. He thought the price certainly
worth paying; but he was much concerned to remind the
supporters of democracy of the danger and the need for
vigilance. "The limitation of the power of government
over individuals loses none of its importance when the
holders of power are regularly accountable to the community—that is to the strongest party therein."[19] So insistent was Mill on this theme that, as Morley said, his
essay was in a sense "one of the most aristocratic books
that ever was written."[20] Certainly Mill's doctrine con-
trasts very sharply with the emphasis placed by Stephen
on the importance in moral matters of public opinion, and
on the function of punishment as an "expression of the
moral sentiment of the public." Morley indeed said, as
Stephen tells us in his Preface,[21] that where Mill would
protect the minority from coercion by the majority, Stephen's principles would expose them to it.

Stephen repudiated Morley's charge, and it was perhaps
unfair. For though Stephen's disclaimer is not very easy
to reconcile with his insistence on the importance of "the
overwhelming moral majority," it may well be that his
complex position does not reduce to anything so simple as

[19] *On Liberty*, Chapter 1.
[20] Quoted in the Preface to *Liberty, Equality, Fraternity*, p. xv.
[21] *Ibid.*, p. xvii.

the view that a popular demand for coercion or legal punishment was justified simply because it was popular or the
cry of the majority. Nonetheless, Mill's fear that such a
doctrine might spread with democracy is surely justified.
It seems fatally easy to believe that loyalty to democratic
principles entails acceptance of what may be termed moral
populism: the view that the majority have a moral right
to dictate how all should live. This is a misunderstanding
of democracy which still menaces individual liberty, and I
shall devote the remainder of this lecture to identifying
the confusion on which it rests.[22]

The central mistake is a failure to distinguish the acceptable principle that political power is best entrusted to
the majority from the unacceptable claim that what the
majority do with that power is beyond criticism and must
never be resisted. No one can be a democrat who does not
accept the first of these, but no democrat need accept the
second. Mill and many others have combined a belief in

[22] There are vestiges of this confusion in Lord Devlin's latest
contribution to the present topic ("Law, Democracy, and Morality,"
loc. cit.). For he there (p. 639) asserts that "in a democracy a legislator will assume that the morals of his society are good and true;
if he does not he should not be playing an active part in government. . . . But he has not to vouch for their goodness and truth.
His mandate is to preserve the essentials of his society, not to re-
construct them according to his own ideas." But elsewhere (p. 644)
he concedes that a legislator "has a very wide discretion in deter-
mining how far he will go in the direction of the law as he thinks
it ought to be." Lord Devlin's main concern in this essay is to estab-

a democracy as the best—or least harmful—form of rule with the passionate conviction that there are many things which not even a democratic government may do. This combination of attitudes makes good sense, because, though a democrat is committed to the belief that democracy is better than other forms of government, he is not committed to the belief that it is perfect or infallible or never to be resisted. To support this last conclusion we need a further premise, going far beyond the simple assertion that it is better to entrust political power to the majority than to a selected class. This further premise must be some variant, secular or otherwise, of the identification of *vox populi* with *vox Dei*. One variant, which has been frequently referred to in these lectures, is the view that positive morality supported by an overwhelming moral majority is immune from criticism.

It is not, of course, surprising that these confusions have been made or that they survive even in democracies like the United States, where the rights of individuals are pro-

---

lish against "the view of the philosophers" (*sic*) that there is no objection to morality being a matter for the popular vote (p. 642), that morality is a question of fact (p. 649), and that in a democracy "educated men cannot be put in a separate category for the decision of moral questions" (p. 643). But as far as positive morality is concerned, few would dispute these contentions. The question remains: What justifies its enforcement by law? As to that, Lord Devlin seems content with his previous arguments and his analogy with treason, criticised above.

tected to some extent from majorities by a written constitution; or in England, where for long the elected member of Parliament has been considered to be the representative but not the delegate of his constituents. For there are in the actual working of democracy many forces likely to encourage the belief that the principle of democratic rule *means* that the majority are always right. Even the most high-minded politician may want to stay in office, and a pliant or passive attitude to what the majority thinks right makes this easier than a stern adherence to the theory that his duty is to do what he thinks right, and then to accept his dismissal if he cannot persuade the majority to retain him. But what is understandable as a temptation to elected legislators may yet be regretted in those not under a similar temptation. Whatever other arguments there may be for the enforcement of morality, no one should think even when popular morality is supported by an "overwhelming majority" or marked by widespread "intolerance, indignation, and disgust" that loyalty to democratic principles requires him to admit that its imposition on a minority is justified.

CONCLUSION

I hope that these three lectures are clear enough and short enough to make a detailed summary unnecessary. Instead I shall say a word in conclusion about the method of argument which I have followed. I have from the beginning assumed that anyone who raises, or is willing to debate, the question whether it is justifiable to enforce morality, accepts the view that the actual institutions of any society, including its positive morality, are open to criticism. Hence the proposition that it is justifiable to enforce morality is, like its negation, a thesis of critical morality requiring for its support some general critical principle. It cannot be established or refuted simply by pointing to the actual practices or morality of a particular society or societies. Lord Devlin, whose thesis I termed the moderate thesis, seems to accept this position, but I have argued that the general critical principle which he deploys, namely, that a society has the right to take any step necessary for its preservation, is inadequate for his purpose. There is no evidence that the preservation of a society requires the enforcement of its morality "as such." His position only appears to escape this criticism by a confused definition of what a society is.

I have also assumed from the beginning that anyone who regards this question as open to discussion necessarily accepts the critical principle, central to all morality, that human misery and the restriction of freedom are evils; for that is why the legal enforcement of morality calls for justification. I then endeavoured to extricate, and to free from ambiguity of statement, the general principles underlying several varieties of the more extreme thesis that the enforcement of morality or its preservation from change were valuable apart from their beneficial consequences in preserving society. These principles in fact invite us to consider as values, for the sake of which we should restrict human freedom and inflict the misery of punishment on human beings, things which seem to belong to the prehistory of morality and to be quite hostile to its general spirit. They include mere outward conformity to moral rules induced simply by fear; the gratification of feelings of hatred for the wrongdoer or his "retributory" punishment, even where there has been no victim to be avenged or to call for justice; the infliction of punishment as a symbol or expression of moral condemnation: the mere insulation from change of any social morality however repressive or barbarous. No doubt I have not *proved* these things not to be values worth their price in human suffering and loss of freedom; it may be enough to have shown what it is that is offered for the price.

SELECTED BIBLIOGRAPHY

GENERAL

Anon. "The Censor as Aedile," *Times Literary Supplement,* August 4, 1961.

Devlin, Lord. *The Enforcement of Morals.* Maccabaean Lecture in Jurisprudence of the British Academy, 1959. Oxford: Oxford University Press, 1959.

———. "Law, Democracy, and Morality," 110 *University of Pennsylvania Law Review* 635 (1962).

Hart, H. L. A. "Immorality and Treason," *The Listener,* July 30, 1959, p. 162.

———. "The Use and Abuse of the Criminal Law," 4 *Oxford Lawyer* 7 (1961).

Hughes, Graham. "Morals and the Criminal Law," 71 *Yale Law Journal* 662 (1962).

Mill, John Stuart. *On Liberty.* London, 1859.

Rostow, Eugene. "The Enforcement of Morals," *Cambridge Law Journal* 174 (1960).

Stephen, James Fitzjames. *Liberty, Equality, Fraternity.* London, 1873. The Preface to the second edition of 1874 is a reply to Morley's defence of Mill in "Mr. Mill's Doctrine of Liberty," *Fortnightly Review,* August 1, 1873.

Stephen, James Fitzjames. *A History of the Criminal Law of England*. London, 1883. Volume II, Chapter 17.

Wollheim, Richard. "Crime, Sin, and Mr. Justice Devlin," *Encounter,* November 1959, p. 34.

LEGAL MATERIAL

American Law Institute, Model Penal Code, Tentative Draft No. 4, 1955.

Davies, D. Seaborne. "The House of Lords and the Criminal Law," *Journal of the Society of Public Teachers of Law* (1961), p. 104.

Goodhart, A. L. "The Shaw Case: The Law and Public Morals," 77 *Law Quarterly Review* 567 (1961).

Jones v. Randall (1774). Lofft. 383.

Report of the Committee on Homosexual Offences and Prostitution (CMD 247) 1957 (The Wolfenden Report).

Shaw v. Director of Public Prosecutions (1961) 2 A.E.R. 446 (1962) A.C. 220.

Williams, Glanville. "Conspiring to Corrupt," *The Listener,* August 24, 1961, p. 275.

Williams, J. E. Hall. "The Ladies Directory and Criminal Conspiracy," 24 *Modern Law Review* 631 (1961).

INDEX

Adultery, 26, 27

American law, 7, 25, 26–27, 39 n., 80

American Law Institute Model Penal Code, 15, 40

Animals: cruelty to, 34

Bentham, Jeremy, 4, 12

Bigamy, 38–43

Blasphemy, 44

Burke, Edmund, 73–75

California, 7, 26–27

Capital punishment, 58, 61, 65

Coercion, 21, 57–58

Consent of victim of crime, 30–34

Conspiracy to corrupt public morals, 6–12

Democracy, 77–81. *See also* Majority opinion

Denning, Lord, 65

Denunciation, 63–66, 83

Devlin, Lord, 16, 18–19, 20 n., 28–32, 34, 38, 41, 48, 49–52, 54, 55, 57, 67, 70, 79 n.

Divine commands, 23, 73

Enforcement of morals, 4–6, 17–18, 21, 25–27, 29, 30–34, 48 *ad fin.*

Fornication, 26–27, 67

Goddard, Lord, 61

Hand, Learned, 15

Harm, 4, 5, 42, 46, 47

Hegel, G. W. F., 73–74

Homosexuality, 9, 13–14, 45, 52, 67–68

Indecency, 38–48

Justice, 3, 37, 60

Justification, 20–21, 82

Justinian, 50

Kelsen, Hans, 3

Lawrence, D. H., 10

Liberty, 21, 22, 46–48

Los Angeles, 27

Majority opinion, 62–63, 67–68, 77–81

Mansfield, Lord, 7, 9

Mill, J. S., 4–6, 14–18, 27–33, 42, 46, 71, 75–77, 78–79

Morality: and law, 1–4; critical, 17, 19–20, 21, 24, 71, 73, 82; positive, 17, 20, 24, 82; value of, 19, 70–74, 83
Morley, J., 28, 78
Natural Law, 2, 23, 73
Obscenity, 10–11
Paternalism, 30–34, 38
Polygamy, 38
Positivism, 2
Prostitution, 8, 11, 13, 14, 26, 45
Punishment: gradation of, 34–38, 58–60. *See also* Denunciation; Enforcement of morals; Justification; Retribution
Reid, Lord, 8, 10
Retribution, 58–61, 83

Rostow, E. V., 38, 42 n.
Sexual morality, 5, 6, 18, 22, 25–27, 67–69. *See also* Adultery; Bigamy; Fornication; Homosexuality; Indecency
Shaw *v* Director of Public Prosecutions, 7–12, 25, 44
Simonds, Lord, 9, 44
Stephen, J. F., 16, 28, 34–38, 48, 55, 57, 60–64, 67, 69, 75–79
Tocqueville, Alexis de, 77
Utilitarianism, 4, 20, 22, 23, 24, 37, 46–47, 55
Utility, 4
Wolfenden Committee: Report of, 13–15, 16, 42
Wollheim, R., 51, 68